*An elegantly simple key to
living a good & thoughtful life*

THE POWER TO LOVE

by Davida Patrick Moore

ThePowerToLove.com
ThinkersAndSinkers.com
DavidaPatrickMoore.com

Cover art inspired by Brian Sisson
Spanish translation by Esmeralda Mariscal and Cristina Barba
All graphics and photography by Davida Patrick Moore

First Edition 2023

Dedication

This book is dedicated to
the process of seeing the
singular Love that is all things.

To those who understand the simplicity
of Love and for those who feel Love,
yet do not fully gather its Power.

For the incarnated soul, this world, and
the Source of Creation are each, and all, the
substance of Love, gathering in and applying
this realization is the difference between
existing in a world and living your life.

Enjoy

Acknowledgements

Thank you for your curiosity in exploring The Power To Love. By exploring this subject, Choosing Love gains a greater prospect as an option for those who thoughtfully want the best for themselves and others.

Brian Sisson was the individual who catalyzed this offering. This book is less-likely to be in the hands of readers without his insights. His editing and rewriting of the original text opens this information to a wider audience. Thanks Big B for encouraging me and for clarifying The Power To Love.

Susanne Westplate, while learning The Power To Love, discovered a dynamic illustration invisible to my eyes. This being the orientation of the hand symbolizing the three paths. Thank you Susi for being that open channel which delivered this powerful teaching tool.

Esmeralda Mariscal and Cristina Barba came to assist the author when having a Spanish language version of this book was merely a daydream. Their combined efforts brought that whimsy to reality. "Gracias, mi amigas," for the support in sharing The Power To Love with an even wider audience.

Thinkers give attention to expressions that uplift the world. Thank you for reading, practicing, and sharing this message of Choosing Love.

Table of Contents

Introduction

If you would like a more uplifted and uplifting life for yourself and those around you then this is the book for you.

In the pursuit of happiness there's the possibility that we will give in before finding our greatest happiness. Seeing beyond the obvious can be challenging.

Our expectations can hold us in place, keeping us from achieving the amazing. If you think you know what your greatest happiness would be, you might be surprised by life, when something truly uplifting and completely beyond your thought process appears only to reshape your perspective forever.

This book is about creating a space in your life for the unexpected and the unspeakably awe-inspiring.

The source through which these realities flow is,
"The Power To Love."

The Purpose

The purpose of this book is to help you uplift your own life. I will show you how to teach yourself to think deeper and to react less from emotion - to be thoughtful instead of thoughtless.

STOP reading right now if want a shaman, priest, savior, pied piper, or someone else that you think will do this for you. You are the only one who can create happiness in your life. You are the only one who can make this happen for yourself.

As you read, I will show you an easier path to greater living. Waiting for you is a new life filled with joy, gratitude, confidence, and consistency. There are no hidden agendas or power plays, no hierarchy, passwords, and zero judgment.

Zero Judgment

The Purpose

I am merely encouraging a new outlook, an elegantly simple key to living a good and thoughtful life. This is done while trusting your own intuition with impersonal neutrality and remaining free from judgment, of yourself and others. It is simple. Though at first it may not be easy in time it can become effortless. You will learn the ability to center your life in an uplifting condition.

Part of this work is to more fully accept that what others do is outside our control. The process is to love ceaselessly and to reflect with great appreciation, gratitude, and happiness for the things in your life.

Endlessly, each day, we are confronted with people, situations, and events that demand our reaction. Our responses define us moment-to-moment and as we respond we turn our lives in one direction or the other, upward, toward more happiness or downward, toward less happiness.

The Purpose

This book can/will guide you to pay close attention to your own reactions and thought process. This will give you the wherewithal to achieve your greatest happiness.

The mission of this book is: "To prompt people to think about how they think." In doing this you may eliminate unnecessary struggle from your life. From that point, unlimited happiness flows. Building upon this way of life will have a ripple effect benefiting countless others.

What is offered here is FREE and liberating:

The Power To Love.

How It All Happens

Countless times every day we are called upon to respond to the world in and around us. We cannot get away from responding. Even doing nothing is a response. Knowing this, it becomes more important to know what motivates our responses.

Our responses to events and circumstances, "come to us," from one of two sources within our being.

The first is from our instinctual self, a source of subconscious determination that has protected humankind for tens of thousands of years. These instincts still serves us greatly in life-or-death situations but often it also overshadows our life with unnecessary displays of egocentric behavior or base cravings.

Unlike our ancient ancestors, most of us don't use our fight-or-flight instincts daily.

How It All Happens

The second source which informs our responses to daily life is our intellectual self, our mind. In humanity, this is a more recent capability, grown out of building civilizations and other thoughtful endeavors over the last several thousand years. This more thoughtful reasoning includes our growing unconditional love for humanity, truth as we see it, wisdom as we know it, and our connection to things greater than ourselves.

This expansion of humanity revolves around love. So, what is love? Here is a definition, "LOVE is a state of mind that has the absence of mental strife, tension, trouble, and envy and is filled with appreciation, gratitude, and happiness." Love uplifts the human condition and is not judgmental. This thoughtful and reflective type of love makes humans unique, but even modern humans need to practice this gift.

To use love as an influential expression, humanity must learn to act and react to life and all situations using our intellectual mind, more so than our instinctual self. This entails some self-training and is where the possibilities for all people to uplift their life experience begins.

In expressing our intellectual mind the instinctual self is first reprogramed and then continually reenforced inline with our thoughtful nature. Over time the instinctual self reflections the intellectual mind.

Let's Get Started

Our actions and words reflect one of only three attitudes: Embracing, Rejecting, or Neutrality. These attitudes can be thought of using the phrases, "I Love It," "I Hate It," and, "Whatever." This is very important. These are your only choices when responding to life.

To gain the benefit here you must begin to stop in the moment, identify the three attitudes, and only THEN should you intellectually chose your reaction to whatever it is you are confronting. This simple guideline accesses The Power To Love.

Here is another definition, "HATE is the lack of love." Hate is an action with misidentified or an obvious absence of love. Hate, also seen as judgment, is the dark element that has produced all of the anguish and unnecessary death in the long history of humanity. Hate is a giant category that is based upon judgment and in short includes all the confused, chaotic, and to use a word, "evil," urges of humankind.

Hate lacks love and in that is thoughtless. It is undesirable and self-destructive. Physical harm, suicide, murder, and emotional/mental abuse are universally undesirable and destructive, as well as, counterproductive to the human spirit and are all products of hate.

Why This Matters

In life there are settings that include our homes, friends, and communities, which contribute to our experience. Each of these settings matches a level of love. Some have more, some have less. In these settings; people, situations, and events are influenced by how much love is around.

When people, situations, and events are exposed to settings with more love there's a greater likelihood they will be uplifted. In settings with less love a feeling of hopelessness, anger, and even rage can develop. As these feelings exist each setting is slowly moved toward more of whatever is predominate in the setting. But this can be changed.

A happy setting can have despair introduced changing the direction things are going. A sad setting can have hope delivered changing that setting. Now this works between people, in situations, and during events. Good things can go bad and bad things can turn good.

Why This Matters

But also, good things can get better and bad things can get worse. It all depends on how much love is brought to and created in each setting. Be careful because sometimes it can be difficult to tell how good or bad things are if you become too accustomed to the feeling in your setting.

When a change of direction is taking place the predominate feeling in a setting will likely experience a period of friction because of the coming change. Good settings will create a push back against a downturn and believe it or not, some bad settings will experience a push back against the feelings of hopefulness and love.

The push back in either case is chosen by the people in the setting. If the people in each setting are thoughtful they will choose love and do without hate and judgment. This can uplift any person, situation, or event inside the setting.

Why This Matters

These settings are happening everywhere people go. It could be between you and a friend, parent, sibling, co-worker, and so on; it could be at work, a social setting, or public space. Because in any interaction between people, we will be choosing between, "I Love It," "I Hate It," and, "Whatever." And in the choosing comes the potential for friction.

But the friction isn't guaranteed, because we can always choose to not engage the friction created by judgment (I hate . . .), or we can choose love or neutrality.

Remember, you can only control yourself and while you might inspire others to choose love, there's really no telling what THEY will do.

That's why it is important to talk about the concept of The Power To Love with everyone and in all avenues of conversation; public and private. By raising awareness more people will become mindful of choosing love. While this will uplift the world, each of us can only do this for ourselves.

The Power To Love

You have the ability (the Power), to choose love over harm and judgment. You create your own uplifting condition when you choose love. You are in control, always and everywhere since you can choose love or reject love.

Your power to love can alter your surroundings and inspire those near you. How? We choose if we stay near darkness and hatred. If we do that, we become more accepting of that darkness to the point we begin to conjure up that behavior from within ourselves.

We can also chose to spin on our heels (mentally and physically), and move away without comment. A few weeks of moving away from hate will change your very environment and draw you toward the company of people who reflect love instead of hate. Yes, it is that simple. Again . . . not always easy.

We can strengthen our Power To Love; all day, every day, 24/7/365.25, by choosing love or neutrality over hate and judgment. Our first option is to always choose neutrality (always), and reflect with appreciation and joy over even the tiniest blessing.

The Power To Love

For many people, this will be difficult, as they may have spent a life counting their debts and logging their hurts and insults. Modern culture justifies this dark behavior; encouraging envy and distrust. The Power To Love can teach you how to forego this response.

Understand that only YOU can better your life. That is your job alone. The world confronts us all ceaselessly with situations, choices, problems, and mayhem. We must react to the destructive with calm, neutral, and un-emotional intellect in order to engage The Power To Love.

Do not search for some entity to take you off the hook. You own your reactions, opinions, and behavior. What you do will continue to create your life experience.

You were born with free will and you may possibly have used counterproductively many times. That's okay, because you are now learning to use your free will wisely. You can become a beacon of good.

The Power To Love

This is the image I want you to remember:

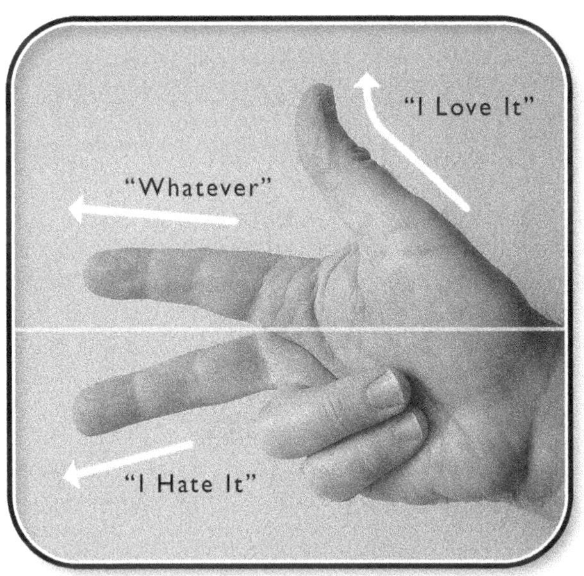

The Power To Love

Yes, very simple. Now let's examine this system. The three fingers represent the three choices mentioned early on: Embracing, Rejecting, and Neutrality, these are your only choices in life. For our purposes, let's use the phrases, "I Love It," "I Hate It," and, "Whatever."

The choice of neutrality, "Whatever," is the new universal word meaning, "Unconcerned." For us, "Whatever," becomes an important choice: "Whatever," means, "I can live with having no opinion of that thing I perceive." (Remember, once anything: person, situation, or event is recognized the person perceiving it must response.) "I am unconcerned because it is not mine to change, it is not mine to control." Changing something is not the same as producing an alternative to something. Replacing something does not change it. It merely puts something else in its place. "Whatever" is accepting that something is the way it is because it belongs to, and the responsibility of, someone else.

"I Hate It"

Hold up your hand as shown. Wiggle your middle finger, the Hate finger. This choice represents all the dark impulses in your mind and the absence of love.

"I Hate It"

Having already shown you the destructive power of hate, I now want you to effectively banish this choice.

That's right, NEVER choose hate once you identify it intellectually as the, "Hate It," choice. Choosing hate does not produce anything of positive value and only degrades the person who chooses it.

Again, simple but not always easy. Many of us have spent a life identifying things we hate. People hang onto it for dear life. We keep old resentments, we harbor hurt feelings of harm or disappointment. You can teach yourself to drop the hate and choose one of the remaining two: "I Love It" or "Whatever."

This you need to do FOR YOUR OWN MENTAL HEALTH and HAPPINESS. Gathering dark thoughts and hatred opens you up to dark forces from lower frequencies. Those instincts can be delicious to indulge, as any criminal in prison can attest.

"I Hate It," is not a valid attitude choice. Ever! Discard it! I mean it! It can be done, and IS intelligently done ceaselessly by wise persons in all walks of life.

"Whatever"

Now look at your hand again, identify the index finger, the "Whatever" choice. "Whatever" is a valid choice. It now takes the place of not only things you can live with, which is most of life, but now it assumes all the old things you once hated; you assign to neutrality all those things you once hated.

This concept is taught by every important religion and has been relayed by mystics since prehistoric times. Simply get over it. Drop your resistance and resentments. You are learning a new life skill, one that brings you true contentment. Release the desire to control; people, situations, and events that are not yours to control.

"I Love It"

Now, the remaining finger, hold up your thumb (I know it's not a finger). Look at it. In the west and in many other places a, "Thumbs Up," is a positive gesture. It means, "I Love It," and you need to teach yourself to be more open to the gentleness of Choosing LOVE. This means you must examine HOW you think . . . often. Realize the appreciable nature in the world around you and in your life.

When you thoughtfully consider what your choices produce you begin to realize the benefits of choosing other than, "I Hate . . ." Being thoughtful is the key. Being thoughtful will help you to choose wisely (thoughtfully).

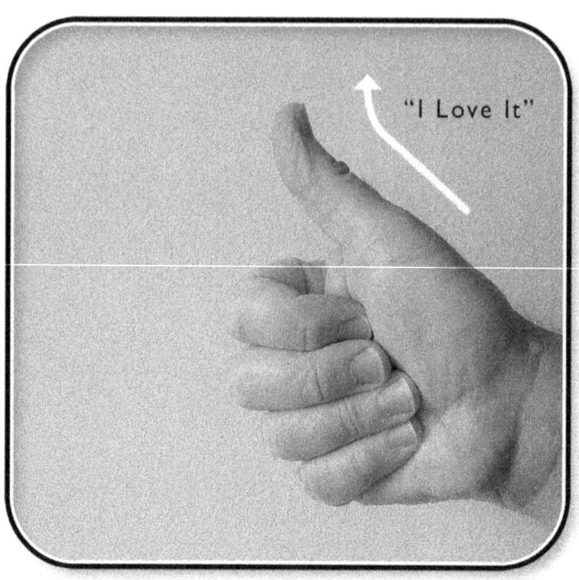

The Technique

Remember, you must teach yourself to chose, "Whatever," or "I Love It," as the answer to every question; the response to every perception. It might be hard, and it takes practice. You must go through the mental exercise each time: Why do I choose hate? Does this cause me friction? Am I resisting something needlessly? If so, identify the impulse and rethink it.

Try out, "Whatever," imagine you don't have a strong opinion against what you used to hate. Does this thing you once objected to REALLY control or destroy your happiness? It really cannot. Nothing means anything until you decide what it means. By choosing, "I Hate It," you reinforce hatred in your life and your surroundings. This supports dark forces.

"You will never end up someplace you didn't go." You cannot avoid this reality. It is mechanical. If you live a life in judgment you will not find yourself in the, "Land of Happiness."
It is not possible.

You can walk away from the influence of dark forces.
You will surprise yourself in a very short time.

One does not move from judgment to love without going through the state of neutrality. Moving from judgment to neutrality is highly productive. Choosing neutrality, "Whatever," is the most productive and realistic choice a person can make when it comes to dealing with anything outside of their power to control. A person only rightfully controls; people, situations, and events for which they are responsible.

The Outcome

You will find yourself happier because you dropped hatreds by the armful. Hate weighs down the mind. It pulls you down to resentment, harm, and emotional abuse.

You will also recognize that many things you once hated were, really, unimportant. You see, you never HAD the power to change most things you once hated and they never really effected you. You now re-file them as "Whatever" (nothing I can do about it, not enough information, unconcerned), or you can realize some value in them and respond with, "I Love It."

You may ask: isn't that just apathy? Let's examine. Turning a small annoying thing you used to hate, say, "housework," into "Whatever" or "I Love It" is a conscious choice to feel better about your world. You can be neutral about doing housework and you can even learn to Love It. There is nothing dreadful about living in a clean house.

What about something important or evil that you hated . . . say fistfights? Isn't it apathetic to relegate "Whatever" or "I Love It" to, "fistfights?" No it is not. Clearly you don't, "love," fistfights and it is counterproductive even if the person getting beat is your rapist or attacker.

The Outcome

As a general attitude about strangers engaged in fighting:
if you are not involved and can DO nothing to stop it, your
smart choice is "Whatever." Most often, participants in a brawl
have the ability to engage or flee. When this is not the case
other remedies are called for. Generally, we all choose how/if we
engage each moment.

This book is not to tell people how to behave, but instead to
show them they only have three choices when they respond to
life. If someone starts a fistfight, they have chosen and actively
succumb to their desire to hate.

Remember this: if you're not causing them, you don't, "allow,"
bad things to happen but you must, "accept," that they happen.
Usually they are beyond your power to allow or disallow. YOU
do not have the ability to dictate all the events around you,
it is for you to accept all things that are beyond your power.
Do not judge.

From there you get to choose how you respond to events by
what you do afterward. You could build something loving and
uplifting to overcome past events, you could remain neutral,
dispassionately unaffected, or you could judge by choosing
hate and create all the degrading and self-destructive behavior
and mindset in that choice.

The Outcome

Nothing means anything until you decide what it means.

Even grand categories such as, "war," cannot be simply dealt with as, "I Hate It." Many wars were waged in order to stop an, "evil," from spreading. Stopping the Hitler war machine was also war, fought for good reason. Teach yourself, re-examine your long-held assumptions about things big and small.

Your internal scorekeeping must be upgraded. There is a growing influence that wants us to hate. I call that mindset the, "Sinker mentality." Look into that concept because it has been growing and is intent upon turning you into a hating machine. **(Read: "Thinkers and Sinkers, Why Are They Trying To Kill You? ISBN 9780615450407)**

If you look around at the world today you can easily see the success of the Sinker mentality. Because you are aware of your connection to unconditional love, truth, wisdom, and bliss you can culture yourself toward those things, uplifting yourself and the world around you.

This is done in the way of the, **"Thinker mindset."**

The Outcome

Now that we know your job is to choose Love or Whatever we must fine tune your decision making so that you do not blindly follow the herd or live in your base instincts.

A little practice will loudly warn you when you are following a less-productive gut reaction, but there is much work needed to improve your critical thinking skills. This is what the Sinker mentality is trying to talk you out of doing.

HERE'S A SIDE NOTE: You may have emotional energy that gets trapped in your body. I know that can sound kinda, "Far Out," yet mystics have known about this for ages and it is something more people are coming to understand. It is very important to learn how to assuage that energy from your body.

Without such techniques you could end up with this trapped energy causing you bodily harm and disease (dis-ease).

Letting go is good enough but if you have difficulties you'll want to make sure you're not hanging on to those old resentments for the above mentioned reason.

Try this for Far Out, holding on to this emotional energy can get encoded into your DNA and passed down through your offspring, promoting the dis-ease.

Thoughtfulness and Thoughtlessness

Critical thinking is the only real thinking. Your ideas, words, and actions are the result of one of the following two approaches: Thoughtfulness and Thoughtlessness. Seems obvious, right? Yet, I submit that many people react/act/discuss/engage from a thoughtless origin . . . assuming that they've come upon their suppositions honestly.

Wait, not so fast! We carry in our minds many opinions that were fed to us without our intellectual investigation. We accepted them as the current logic, or the vast public opinion, or perhaps we learned them from parents, friends, teachers, or the media.

Previously, in my own life, I was in marketing and promotions. It is a modern science of consensus-making that is clever and insidious. I learned that the, "consumer," as a type, reacts emotionally to messages. Consumers are really just ALL OF US taken as a prototype. People as a group form opinions based on things both profound AND silly.

We tend to go along with the crowd (the herd), so as not to upset people around us. Whether we are aware of this or not, we tend to agree with the clique we wish to be counted amongst.

In order for you to sharpen your critical thinking, you must THINK about how you think. Read that again as many times as it takes to make sense.

Thoughtfulness and Thoughtlessness

Many people are fountains of information and speech which they confidently espouse, but about which they have given almost no thought. Preconceived notions abound, indeed they constitute the largest mass of opinion and attitude in our world.

Rare is the sage who muses through each thought looking for truth and cohesion. Centuries ago there were people of that sort, they were intellectual and thoughtful, living monastic lives.

In our hurry-up modern world, we must make ourselves thoughtfully digest information and opinions on the fly, slowing down only for important bits as we gape at the continuing river of daily information. It's not impossible! With the internet, and at the snap of a keystroke, we are all tapped into the equivalent of the great libraries of antiquity.

Though again, our thoughtful and discerning mind must be sharpened and brought to bear to separate the wheat from the chaff, the true and honest knowledge from the propaganda. It's all there.

There is a world of scholarship available to you in order to sharpen your mind.

But keep this in mind: Learning HOW to think is only one of the necessary steps to greater fulfillment.

Thoughtfulness and Thoughtlessness

Keys to Thinking:

Learn to identify hidden sales pitches.

Learn to identify the thoughtless.

Explore the edges of the herd.

Don't assume the experts are right.

Don't give into the accepted notions of the herd.

Run your own self tests, peek behind the curtains.

Reject emotional appeals, they are fool's logic.

Reject dark appeals to envy or hatred, they are unfair and self-destructive.

Research on your own, don't, "accept the premise."

When the whole room agrees, stop and wonder if there is coercion.

When the herd laughs in unison, be wary.

If you don't have enough info to speak, say so.

Ask for clarification, it drives the thoughtless crazy.

And stop judging! This will cloud your thought process and limit your potential.

Thoughtfulness and Thoughtlessness

The above instructions are actually the important tenets of Self Education, the intense learning that can be attained after your school years. Even my friends with advanced post graduate degrees must relearn HOW to think. Many, "college educated," adults have not learned any of the KEYS to THINKING skills listed above.

With a few days practice, you can accurately identify the thoughtful and the thoughtless. Within a year you will be a beacon of (and a magnet for), good vibes.

In the real world, Thoughtfulness is just as hard to find among the college degreed as it is with the blue collar workers. Linear, critical thinking is your only hope of seeing through the modern information smokescreen. Critical thinking, coupled with a healthy spiritual mind, is what informs The Power To Love.

Think clearly in order to Love fully.

Now that you are steeped in the language of both Love and Thinking, let's wrap it up.

How The Power To Love Works

The Power To Love works by seeing beyond fearfully misidentified markers of shortcomings; by viewing without judgment what the ego objects to; and in identifying purpose and providence all around you. We are the conduits of the Infinite Love of . . . (fill in the blank). Whatever you want to call the source of our creation doesn't matter. What matters is how you conceive and perceive the world around you and how you choose to respond to it.

In your life you will encounter all types of people, situations, and events, each matching and vibrating to a level of love. In responding to what is around you, and after time, you will either raise or lower you personal level of love to match that which you encounter for a prolonged period.

If you hold fast to your level of love, the people, situations, or events you encounter will move to match your level. If neither you nor what you encounter changes there will be a split. This is because there isn't a matching of levels and the disharmony becomes too great. This produces the split. If no split occurs the discomfort will simply continue until a split or a merging.

We choose how much love we live with, all day, every day. We choose if we love in the same way as we had previously. As you live your life you choose to be like (or unlike), that which you encounter.

How The Power To Love Works

Two people can watch a simple moment: a toddler sharing a treat with his baby sister, for instance. One views the moment as a precious example of the human capacity for love . . . while the other sees only empty cuteness and remarks that these two sibling will some day fight bitterly with each other.

Both our observers chose their reaction, consciously or not. I posit that you should focus your mind to choose the first, loving reaction, if you aren't simply neutral. It does nothing positive for you or others to be judgmental. Love is the beneficial consciousness of the human soul. Love evolves humankind universally upward to light and truth.

People are the channels through which universal love is made manifest. This is a transcendent quality of human life. This quality is an anathema to the Sinker mentality, which has as its goal (known by many and unknown by most), to debase the transcendent quality of love.

How The Power To Love Works

The Sinker mentality is a part of nature, though undesirable, as it is counterproductive and self-destructive. What you must ask yourself is whether you will support the Sinker mentality by supporting hate and judgment or if you will support the Thinker mindset by Choosing Love and in that choice if you will live a happy and uplifted life.

The choice we all have is to, **"Choose LOVE"** This is a catch phrase I developed so we can speak this entire concept of The Power To Love simply by promoting this form of thoughtfulness. Consider the benefits when you, "Choose LOVE," and you will see the elegantly simple key to living a good and thoughtful life. Neutrality is a form of Love. Being neutral, allows for "space" in which the less thoughtful can evaluate their current process. Being neutral, in most cases, denies the judgmental something to rail against.

The image of a hand holding up those particular three finger is a reminder of the choices each person has in responding to the world. This iconic communication quickly reminders everyone there are only three choices with which to response to their perceptions. ("I Love It," "I Hate It," or "Whatever")

How The Power To Love Works

Here is a simple dialog one can use to start a conversation discussing the idea of, **"Choosing LOVE."**

Let's say you've just seen someone act in a way that would best be described as thoughtless. If they seem approachable and there is no threat of physical violence, you can talk to them, quietly, one-on-one, and this is how things might go:

You: Hey (spoken calmly), do you know what this is? (You ask this holding up three fingers. Now the thoughtless individual has the same three choices they will ever have as you stand in front of them holding up your hand.)

Them: No, what do you mean? (Listening to their voice you will either hear, "I Love It," "I Hate It," or "Whatever.")

You: This is magic. Would you like to learn the magic that will create boundless happiness in your life?

Them: (Again, they are prompted to answer your question and they will, from the three choices.) Okay. (Is one option and again you can hear their disposition in the tone of their voice. The only other thing they can say is, "No.")

How The Power To Love Works

You: This is a reminder that whenever we respond to things around us, our actions will be either embracing, rejecting, or neutral. Now the magic is found in remembering that when we reject we diminish ourselves. Rejecting someone, something, or a situation degrades us by creating resistance and friction. People get use to it but it still drags us down and it doesn't have to be that way. We can do positive uplifting things that will bring us more happiness. I know, that sounds kinda trippy but how else can we describe it? Being judgmental cannot create happiness.

This is when you give them a smile. The concept is this will help them think about how they think. You've done your part.

THAT'S THE WHOLE STORY, PRACTICE MAKES PERFECT AND ONCE YOU'VE MOVED AWAY FROM CHOOSING JUDGMENT, "I HATE," YOU WILL SEE THINGS THAT USE TO BOTHER YOU IN A WHOLE NEW LIGHT, OR NOT AT ALL. WHEN WE LOOK TO UPLIFT EVERYTHING AROUND US OUR HAPPINESS WILL NATURALLY EXPAND.

You, and the world, benefit as you are embracing, engaging, and embodying **The Power To Love.**

Thank you.

Davida Patrick Moore (the author)

As an esoteric consultant, Davida Patrick Moore plies the trades
of divination, meditation, and energy healing, along with consulting
and training in the realms of manifestation, personal energy system
management, and most pointedly in societal and cultural dynamics.

Professional Astrologer, Tarotist, and
certified Pranic Healer, are clarified
in Davida's bio. Other credits include;
rock/pop, jazz, and classical musician,
esoteric trainer/coach, public speaker,
and published author.

Aware in the 1960s, Davida's interest
in the esoteric and cosmic were natural
expressions from an early age. In his
youth, ancient civilizations struck a
chord within Davida; culture, language,
and myth were curious attractions.

A rough outline of engagement runs
from classical music, meditation, and

Davida Patrick Moore

astrology/tarot, through spiritual philosophy, publishing,
and public speaking, to energy healer, esoteric coach and trainer.

"Thinkers and Sinkers, Why Are They Trying To Kill You?" Davida's 2011
book, (ThinkersAndSinkers.com), outlines the interpersonal patterns
found on every level of life and at the crux of the modern experience.
The expression of belligerent intent found throughout the social and
personal landscapes exposes the existential struggle against Universal
Love by Chaos. Revealing this self-destructive influence is prime to
Davida's life efforts. Supporting Spiritual Growth and Self Healing are
the central focus of these efforts.

Una Clave Elegantemente Simple Para Vivir una Buena Vida y una Vida Reflexiva

EL PODER DE AMAR

por Davida Patrick Moore

ThePowerToLove.com
ThinkersAndSinkers.com
DavidaPatrickMoore.com (solo inglés)

Portada inspirada en Brian Sisson
Traducción al español por Esmeralda Mariscal y Cristina Barba
Todos los gráficos y fotografías por Davida Patrick Moore

Primera Edición 2023

Dedicatoria

Este libro está dedicado al proceso de ver
el Amor singular que es todas las cosas.

Para aquellos que entienden la simplicidad
del Amor y para aquellos que sienten Amor,
pero no reúnen plenamente su Poder.

Para el alma encarnada, este mundo y la Fuente
de la Creación son cada uno, y todos, la sustancia
del Amor, reunirse y aplicar esta realización es
la diferencia entre existir en un mundo y vivir tu vida.

Agradecimientos

Gracias por su curiosidad en explorar El Poder De Amar. Al explorar este tema, Elegir el Amor gana una perspectiva más grande como una opción para aquellos que desean lo mejor para sí mismos y para los demás.

Brian Sisson fue el individuo que catalizó esta oferta. Es menos probable que este libro esté en manos de los lectores sin sus ideas. Su edición y reescritura del texto abre esta información a un público más amplio. Gracias Big B por animarme y por aclarar El Poder De Amar.

Susanne Westplate, mientras aprendía El Poder De Amar, descubrió una ilustración dinámica invisible para mis ojos. Siendo esta la orientación de la mano que simboliza los tres caminos. Gracias Susi por ser ese canal abierto que entregó esta poderosa herramienta de enseñanza.

Esmeralda Mariscal y Cristina Barba vinieron a ayudar al autor cuando tener una versión en español de este libro era simplemente un sueño. Sus esfuerzos combinados trajeron esa fantasía a la realidad. Gracias mis amigas por el apoyo para compartir The Power To Love con una audiencia aún más amplia.

Los pensadores de prestan atención a las expresiones que elevan el mundo. Gracias por leer, practicar y compartir este mensaje de Elegir el Amor.

Tabla de Contenido

Introducción

Si desea una vida mas elevada y edificante para usted y
los que lo rodean, entonces este es el libro para usted.

En la búsqueda de la felicidad existe la probabilidad de
que nos rindamos antes de encontrar nuestra mayor felicidad.
Ver más allá de lo obvio puede ser un desafío. Nuestras
expectativas pueden mantenernos en su lugar, impidiéndonos
lograr lo asombroso. Si crees que sabes cual seria tu mayor
felicidad, es posible que te sorprenda la vida cuando algo
más allá de tu proceso de pensamiento aparece solo para
remodelar tu perspectiva para siempre.

Este libro trata de crear un espacio en tu vida para lo
inesperado y lo indescriptiblemente inspirador.

La fuente a través de la cual fluyen estas realidades es
"El Poder De Amar."

El Propósito

El propósito de este libro es ayudarte a elevar tu propia
vida. Te mostrare como enseñarte a ti mismo a pensar más
profundamente y reaccionar menos antes las emociones,
a ser reflexivo en lugar de irreflexivo.

DEJA de leer ahora mismo si quieres un Chamán, sacerdote,
salvador, flautista deHamelin, o alguien mas que creas que hará
esto por ti. Eres el único que puede crear felicidad en tu vida.
Eres la única que puede a ver que esto suceda por ti mismo.

A medida que lea, le mostrare un camino más fácil hacia una
vida mejor. Te espera una nueva vida llena de alegría, gratitud,
confianza y constancia. No hay agendas ocultas ni juegos de
poder, ni jerarquías, ni contraseñas, ni juicios.

El Propósito

Simplemente estoy alentando una nueva perspectiva, una clave simple para vivir una buena vida y reflexiva. Esto se hace mientras confías en tu propia intuición con neutralidad impersonal y te mantienes libre de juicio, de ti mismo y de los demás. Es simple. Aunque al principio puede no ser fácil, con el tiempo puede volverse sin esfuerzo.

Aprenderás la habilidad de centrar tu vida en una condición edificante. Parte de este trabajo es aceptar mas plenamente que lo que hacen los demás esta fuera de tu control. El proceso es amar sin cesar y reflexionar con gran aprecio, gratitud y felicidad por las cosas en tu vida.

Sin cesar, cada día, nos enfrentamos a personas, situaciones y eventos que exigen nuestra reacción. Nuestras respuestas nos definen momento a momento y, a medida que respondemos, giramos nuestras vidas en una dirección u otra, hacia arriba, hacia más felicidad o hacia abajo, hacia menos felicidad.

El Propósito

Este libro puede/te guiará para que prestes mucha atención a tus propias reacciones y procesos de pensamiento. Esto te dará los medios para alcanzar tu mayor felicidad.

La misión de este libro es: "Incitar a las personas a pensar acerca de como piensan." Al hacer esto, puedes eliminar la lucha innecesaria de tu vida. A partir de ese punto fluye una felicidad ilimitada. Construir sobre esta forma de vida tendrá un efecto dominó que beneficiará a muchos otros.

Lo que se ofrece aquí es GRATIS y liberador:
El Poder De Amar.

Cómo Sucede Todo

Incontables veces todos los días somos llamados a responder al mundo dentro y alrededor de nosotros. Nosotros no podemos escapar de responder. Incluso nohacer nada es una respuesta. Sabiendo esto, se vuelve más importante saber que motiva nuestras respuestas.

Nuestras respuestas a los eventos y circunstancias "vienen a nosotros," de una de dos fuentes dentro de nuestro ser.

El primero proviene de nuestro yo instintivo, una fuente de determinación subconsciente que ha protegido a la humanidad durante decenas de miles de año. Estos instintos todavía nos sirven mucho en situaciones de vida o muerte, pero a menudo también eclipsan nuestra vida con demonstraciones innecesarias de comportamiento egocéntrico o anhelos básicos.

A diferencia de nuestros ancestros, la mayoría de nosotros no usamos nuestros instintos de lucha o huida a diario.

Cómo Sucede Todo

La segunda fuente que informa nuestras respuestas a la vida diaria es nuestro ser intelectual, nuestra mente. En la humanidad, esta es una capacidad más reciente, surgida de la construcción de civilizaciones y otros esfuerzos reflexivos durante los últimos miles de año. Este razonamiento más reflexivo incluye nuestro creciente amor incondicional por la humanidad, la verdad tal como la vemos, la sabiduría tal como la conocemos y nuestra conexión con cosas más grandes que nosotros mismos.

Esta expansión de la humanidad gira en torno al amor. Entonces, ¿Qué es el amor? Aquí hay una definición, "AMOR es un estado mental que tiene la ausencia de conflicto mental, tensión, problemas y envidia y esta lleno de aprecio, gratitud y felicidad." El amor eleva la condición humana y no es crítica/o. Este tipo de amor considerado y reflexivo hace que los humanos sean únicos, pero incluso los humanos modernos necesitan practicar este don.

Para usar el amor como una expresión influyente, la humanidad debe aprender a actuar y reaccionar ante la vida y todas las situaciones usando nuestra mente intelectual, más que nuestro yo instintivo. Esto implica algo de autoformación y es donde comienza las posibilidades de que todas las personas eleven su experiencia de vida.

Al expresar nuestra mente intelectual, el yo instintivo primero se reprograma y luego se refuerza continuamente en línea con nuestra naturaleza reflexiva. Con el tiempo, el yo instintivo refleja la mente intelectual.

Empecemos

Nuestras acciones y palabras reflejan una de solo tres actitudes: Abrazar, Rechazar o Neutralidad. Se puede pensar en estas actitudes usando las frases "Me Encanta," "Lo Odio," y "Lo Que Sea." Esto es muy importante. Estas son sus únicas opciones al responder a la vida.

Para obtener el beneficio aquí, debe comenzar a detenerse en el momento, identificar las tres actitudes, y solo ENTONCES debe elegir intelectualmente su reacción a Lo Que Sea que este confrontando. Esta sencilla guía accede a El Poder De Amar.

Aquí hay otra definición, "ODIO es la falta de amor." El odio es una acción con una identificación errónea o una ausencia evidente de amor. El odio visto también como juicio, es el elemento oscuro que ha producido todas las angustias y muertes innecesarias en la larga historia de la humanidad. El odio es una categoría gigante que se basa en el juicio y, en resumen, incluye todos los impulsos confusos, caóticos y, para usar una palabra, "malvados" de la humanidad.

El odio carece de amor y en eso es irreflexivo. Es indeseable y autodestructivo. El daño físico, el suicidio, el asesinato y el abuso emocional/mental son universalmente indeseables y destructivos, así como contraproducentes para el espíritu humano y son todos productos del odio.

Por Que Esto Es Importante

En la vida hay escenarios que incluyen nuestros hogares, amigos y comunidades, que contribuyen a nuestra experiencia. Cada una de estas configuraciones coincide con un nivel de amor. Algunos tienen más, otros tienen menos. En estos entornos; l as personas, las situaciones y los eventos están influenciados por la cantidad de amor que hay alrededor.

Cuando las personas, las situaciones y los eventos se exponen a ambientes con más amor, existe una mayor probabilidad de que se sientan animados. En entornos con menos amor, se puede desarrollar un sentimiento de desesperanza, ira e incluso rabia. A medida que existen estos sentimientos, cada escenario se mueve lentamente hacia más de Lo Que Sea que predomine en el escenario. Peroesto se puede cambiar.

Un entorno feliz puede tener desesperación introducida cambiando la dirección en que van las cosas. Un entorno triste puede recibir esperanza cambiando el entorno. Ahora bien, esto funciona entre personas, en situaciones y durante eventos. Las cosas buenas pueden salir mal y las cosas malas pueden volverse buenas.

Por Que Esto Es Importante

Pero también, las cosas buenas pueden mejorar y las cosas buenas pueden mejorar y las cosas malas pueden empeorar. Todo depende de cuanto amor se traiga y se cree en cada sesión. Tengo cuidado porque a veces puede ser difícil saber que tan buenas o malas son las cosas si se acostumbra demasiado a la sensación en su entorno.

Cuando se esta produciendo un cambio de dirección, es probable que el sentimiento predominante en un escenario experimente un periodo de fricción, debido al cambio que se avecina. Las buenas configuraciones crearan un retroceso contra una recesión y lo creas o no, algunas malas configuraciones experimentaran un retroceso contra los sentimientos de esperanza y amor.

El retroceso en cualquier caso es elegido por las personas en el entorno. Si las personas en cada entorno son reflexivas, elegirán el amor y prescindirán del odio y el juicio. Esto puede animar a cualquier persona, situación o evento dentro del entorno.

Por Que Esto Es Importante

Estos ajustes están ocurriendo donde quiera que vaya la gente. Podría ser entre usted y un amigo, padre, hermano, compañero de trabajo, etc.; podría ser en el trabajo, un entorno social o un espacio público. Porque en cualquier interacción entre personas, estaremos eligiendo entre "Me Encanta," "Lo Odio," y "Lo Que Sea." Y en la elección viene el potencial de fricción.

Pero la fricción no está garantizada, porque siempre podemos optar por no involucrarnos en la fricción creada por el juicio (Odio…), o podemos elegir el amor o la neutralidad.

Recuerda, solo puedes controlarte a ti mismo y, si bien puedes inspirar a otros a elegir el amor, realmente no se sabe lo que ELLOS harán.

Por eso es importante hablar del concepto de El Poder de Amar con todos y en todas las vías de conversación; pública y privada. Al aumentar la conciencia, más personas se volverán consientes de elegir amor. Si bien esto elevara al mundo, cada uno de nosotros solo puede hacerlo por si mismo.

El Poder De Amar

Tu tienes la habilidad (El Poder), de elegir el amor sobre el daño
y el juicio. Creas tu propia condición edificante cuando eliges
el amor. Tienes el control, siempre y en todas partes, ya que
puedes elegir el amor o rechazar el amor.

Tu poder para amar puede alterar tu entorno e inspirar a
quienes te rodean. ¿Cómo? Elegimos si nos quedamos cerca
de la oscuridad y el odio. Si hacemos eso, aceptamos más esa
oscuridad hasta el punto de que comenzamos a evocar ese
comportamiento desde dentro de nosotros mismos.

También podemos optar por girar sobre nuestros talones
(mental y físicamente), y alejarnos sin hacer comentarios.
Unas pocas semanas de alejarte del odio cambiaran tu propio
entorno y te acercaran a la compañía de personas que reflejan
amor en lugar de odio. Si, es así de simple. De nuevo . . .
no siempre es fácil.

Podemos fortalecer nuestro Poder de Amar; todo el día, todos
los días, 24/7/365.25, eligiendo el amor o la neutralidad sobre
el odio y el juicio. Nuestra primera opción es elegir siempre la
neutralidad (siempre), y reflexionar con aprecio y alegría hasta
por la más pequeña bendición.

El Poder De Amar

Para muchas personas, esto será difícil, ya que pueden haber pasado la vida contando sus deudas y registrando sus heridas e insultos. La cultura moderna justifica este oscuro comportamiento; fomentando la envidia y la desconfianza. El Poder De Amar puede enseñarte como renunciar a esta respuesta.

Entiende que solo TU puedes mejorar tu vida. Ese es tu trabajo solo. El mundo nos confronta a todos incesantemente con situaciones, elecciones, problemas y caos. Debemos reaccionar ante lo destructivo con un intelecto tranquilo, neutral y sin emociones para poder comprometer El Poder De Amar.

No busques alguna entidad que te saque del apuro. Eres dueño de tus reacciones, opiniones y comportamiento. Lo que hagas continuara creando tu experiencia de vida.

Naciste con libre albedrio y es posible que lo hayas usado de manera contraproducente muchas veces. Esta bien, porque ahora estas aprendiendo a usar tu libre albedrio sabiamente. Puedes convertirte en un faro del bien.

El Poder De Amar

Esta es la imagen que quiero que recuerdes:

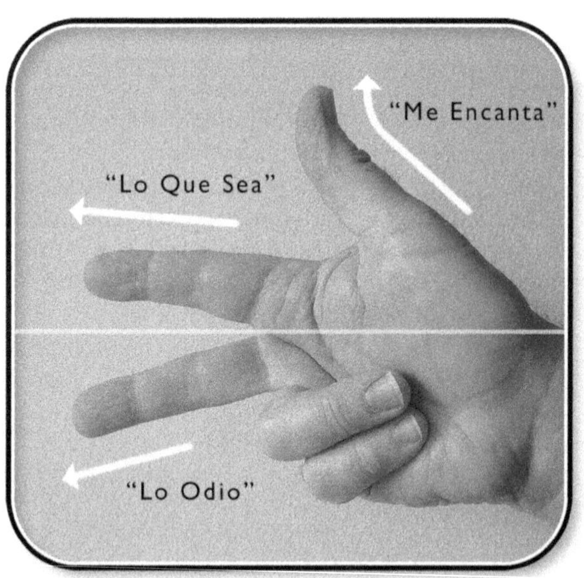

El Poder De Amar

Si, muy sencillo. Ahora examinemos este sistema. Los tres dedos representan las tres opciones mencionadas anteriormente: Abrazar, Rechazar y Neutralidad, estas son sus únicas opciones en la vida. Para nuestros propósitos, usemos las frases "Me Encanta," "Lo Odio," y "Lo Que Sea."

La elección de la neutralidad, "Lo Que Sea," es la nueva palabra universal que significa "Despreocupado." Para nosotros, Lo Que Sea, se convierte en una elección importante: Lo Que Sea, significa "Puedo vivir sin tener una opinión sobre lo que percibo." (Recuerde, una vez que se reconoce cualquier cosa: persona, situación, o evento, la otra persona que lo percibe debe responder). "No me preocupo porque no es mío para cambiar, no es mío para controlar." Cambiar algo no es lo mismo que producir una alternativa a algo. Reemplazar algo no lo cambia. Simplemente pone algo más en su lugar. "Lo Que Sea" es aceptar que algo es como es porque pertenece y es responsabilidad de otra persona.

Lo Odio

Levanta la mano como se muestra. Mueve tu dedo medio,
el dedo del Odio. Esta elección representa todos los impulsos
oscuros en tu mente y la ausencia de amor.

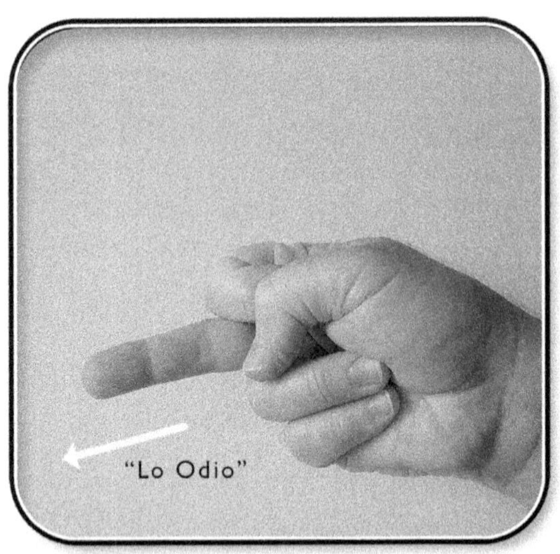

"Lo Odio"

Habiéndote mostrado ya el poder destructivo del odio, ahora quiero que elimines efectivamente esta elección.

Así es, NUNCA elijas el odio una vez que lo identifiques intelectualmente como la opción "Lo Odio." Elegir el odio no produce nada de valor positivo y solo degrada a la persona que lo elige.

Nuevamente, simple pero no siempre fácil. Muchos de nosotros pasamos la vida identificando cosas que odiamos. La gente se aferra a el por su vida. Guardamos viejos resentimientos, albergamos sentimientos heridos de daño o decepción. Puedes enseñarte a ti mismo a dejar el odio y elegir uno de los dos restantes: "Me Encanta" o "Lo Que Sea."

Esto necesitas hacer PARA TU PROPIA SALUD MENTAL y FELICIDAD. Reunir pensamientos oscuros y odio te abre a las fuerzas de abajo. Esos instintos pueden ser deliciosos para complacer, como cualquier criminal en prisión puede atestiguar.

"Lo Odio," no es una opción de actitud validad. ¡Nunca! ¡Deséchalo! ¡En serio! Se puede hacer, y ES inteligentemente hecho incesantemente por personas sabias en todos los ámbitos de la vida.

"Lo Que Sea"

Ahora mira tu mano de nuevo, identifica el dedo índice, la opción Lo Que Sea. Lo Que Sea una elección valida. Ahora toma el lugar no solo de las cosas con las que puedes vivir, que es la mayor parte de la vida, sino que ahora resume todas las cosas viejas que una vez odiaste; asignas a la neutralidad todas esas cosas que alguna vez odiaste.

Este concepto es enseñado por todas las religiones importantes y ha sido transmitido por los místicos desde tiempos prehistóricos. Simplemente superarlo. Abandona tu resistencia y resentimientos. Estas aprendiendo una nueva habilidad para la vida, una que te trae verdadera satisfacción. Libera el deseo de controlar, personas, situaciones y eventos que no son tuyos para controlar.

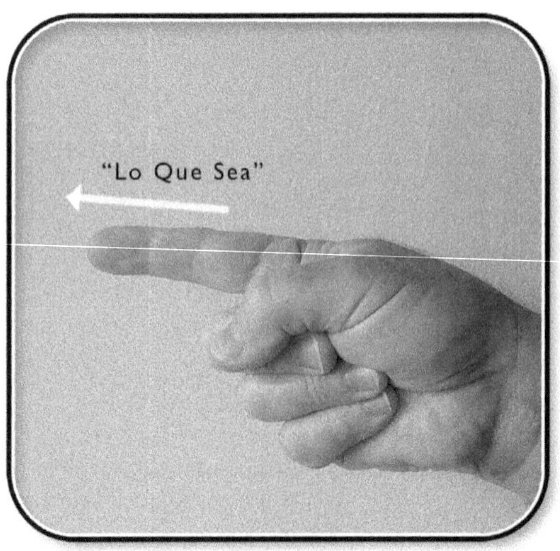

"Me Encanta"

Ahora, el dedo restante, levanta el pulgar, (se que no es un dedo). Míralo. En el oeste y en muchos otros lugares, un "Pulgar Hacia Arriba" es un gesto positivo. Significa, "Me Encanta," y necesitas enseñarte a ti mismo a estar mas abierto a la dulzura de Elegir el Amor. Esto significa que debes examinar COMO piensas . . . a menudo. Date cuenta de la naturaleza apreciable en el mundo que te rodea y en tu vida.

Cuando considera cuidadosamente lo que producen sus elecciones, comienza a darse cuenta de los beneficios de elegir algo que no sea "Lo Odio . . ." Ser pensativo es la clave. Ser reflexivo te ayudara a elegir sabiamente (consideradamente).

La Técnica

Recuerda, debes enseñarte a ti mismo a elegir "Lo Que Sea," o "Me Encanta" como respuesta a cada pregunta; la respuesta a cada precepción. Puede ser difícil y requiere práctica. Tu debes hacer ejercicios mentales cada vez: ¿Por qué elijo el odio? ¿Esto me causa fricción? ¿Me estoy resistiendo a algo innecesariamente? Si es así, identifica el impulso y repiénsalo.

Prueba, "Lo Que Sea," imagina que no tienes una opinión fuerte en contra de lo que solías odiar. ¿Esta cosa a la que alguna vez objetaste REALMENTE controla o destruye tu felicidad? Realmente no puede. Nada significa nada hasta que decidas lo que significa. Al elegir, "Lo Odio," refuerzas el odio en tu vida y en tu entorno. Esto apoya e las fuerzas oscuras.

"Nunca terminaras en un lugar al que no fuiste." No puedes evitar esta realidad. Es mecánico. Si vives una vida en el juicio no te encontraras en la "Tierra de la Felicidad."

No es posible.

Puedes alejarte de la influencia de las fuerzas oscuras. Te sorprenderás en muy poco tiempo.

No se pasa del juicio al amor sin pasar por el estado de neutralidad. Pasar del juicio a la neutralidad es altamente productivo. Elegir la neutralidad, "Lo Que Sea," es la elección más productiva y realista que una persona puede hacer cuando se trata de lidiar con algo que esta fuera de su control. Una persona solo controla legítimamente; personas, situaciones y eventos de los que son responsables.

El Resultado

Te encontrarás más feliz porque soltaste los odios. El odio pesa sobre la mente. Te arrastra hacia el resentimiento, el daño y el abuso emocional.

También reconocerás que muchas cosas que alguna vez odiaste eran, realmente, poco importantes. Verás, nunca tuviste el poder de cambiar la mayoría de las cosas que alguna vez odiaste y nunca te afectaron realmente. Ahora los vuelve a archivar como "Lo Que Sea" (nada que pueda hacer al respecto, no hay suficiente información, sin preocuparse), o puede darse cuenta de algún valor en ellos y responder con: "Me Encanta".

Usted puede preguntar: ¿no es eso sólo apatía? Examinemos. Convertir una pequeña cosa molesta que solías odiar, digamos, "tareas domésticas", en "Lo Que Sea" o "Me Encanta" es una elección consciente para sentirte mejor con tu mundo. Puedes ser neutral acerca de hacer las tareas domésticas e incluso puedes aprender a amarlo. No hay nada terrible en vivir en una casa limpia.

¿Qué pasa con algo importante o malo que odiabas? . . ¿Decir peleas a puñetazos? ¿No es apático relegar "Lo Que Sea" o "Me Encanta" a "peleas a puñetazos"? No, no lo es. Claramente no lo haces, "amas", peleas a puñetazos y es contraproducente incluso si la persona que está siendo golpeada es tu violador o atacante.

El Resultado

Como actitud general sobre los extraños involucrados en peleas: si no estás involucrado y no puedes hacer nada para detenerlo, tu elección inteligente es "Lo Que Sea". Cada participante en una pelea tiene la libertad de participar o huir. Todos elegimos cómo/si nos involucramos en cada momento.

Este libro no es para decirle a la gente cómo comportarse, sino para mostrarles que solo tienen tres opciones cuando responden a la vida. Si alguien comienza una pelea a puñetazos, ha elegido y sucumbe activamente a su deseo de odiar.

Recuerda esto: si no los estás causando, no "permites" que sucedan cosas malas, pero debes "aceptar" que sucedan. Por lo general, están más allá de su poder para permitir o rechazar. TÚ no tienes la capacidad de dictar todos los eventos a tu alrededor, es para que aceptes todas las cosas que están más allá de tu poder. No juzgues.

A partir de ahí, puedes elegir cómo responder a los eventos por lo que haces después. Podrías construir algo amoroso y edificante para superar eventos pasados, podrías permanecer neutral, desapasionadamente no afectado, o podrías juzgar eligiendo el odio y crear todo el comportamiento y la mentalidad degradantes y autodestructivos en esa elección.

El Resultado

Nada significa nada hasta que decidas lo que significa.

Incluso las grandes categorías como "guerra" no pueden ser tratadas simplemente como "Lo Odio". Se libraron muchas guerras para evitar que un "mal" se extendiera. Detener la máquina de guerra de Hitler también fue una guerra, luchada por una buena razón. Enséñate a ti mismo, reexamina tus suposiciones de larga data sobre cosas grandes y pequeñas.

Su puntuación interna debe actualizarse. Hay una influencia creciente que quiere que odiemos. Yo llamo a esa mentalidad la "mentalidad del hundidor". Mira ese concepto porque ha estado creciendo y tiene la intención de convertirte en una máquina de odio. **(Lea: "Thinkers and Sinkers, Why Are They Trying To Kill You? ISBN 9780615450407)** (solo inglés)

Si miras alrededor del mundo de hoy, puedes ver fácilmente su éxito. Debido a que eres consciente de tu conexión con el amor incondicional, la verdad, la sabiduría y la dicha, puedes cultivarte hacia esas cosas, elevándote a ti mismo y al mundo que te rodea. Esto se hace en el camino de la **"mentalidad de pensador"**.

El Resultado

Ahora que sabemos que tu trabajo es elegir Amor o Lo que sea, debemos afinar tu toma de decisiones para que no sigas ciegamente a la manada o vivas en tus instintos básicos.

Un poco de práctica te advertirá en voz alta cuando estés siguiendo una reacción visceral menos productiva, pero hay mucho trabajo necesario para mejorar tus habilidades de pensamiento crítico. Esto es lo que la mentalidad Sinker está tratando de convencerte de que no hagas.

AQUÍ HAY UNA NOTA AL MARGEN: Es posible que tenga energía emocional que quede atrapada en su cuerpo. Sé que puede sonar un poco "Far Out", sin embargo, los místicos han sabido sobre esto durante años y es algo que más personas están llegando a entender. Es muy importante aprender a absorber esa energía de tu cuerpo.

Sin tales técnicas, podrías terminar con esta energía atrapada causándote daño corporal y enfermedad (enfermedad).

Dejar ir es lo suficientemente bueno, pero si tienes dificultades, querrás asegurarte de no aferrarte a esos viejos resentimientos por la razón mencionada anteriormente.

Prueba esto para Far Out, aferrarse a esta energía emocional puede codificarse en tu ADN y transmitirse a través de tu descendencia, promoviendo la enfermedad.

Consideración e Inconsideración

El pensamiento crítico es el único pensamiento real. Sus ideas, palabras y acciones son el resultado de uno de los siguientes dos enfoques: consideración y falta de consideración. Parece obvio, ¿verdad? Sin embargo, sostengo que muchas personas reaccionan / actúan / discuten / se involucran desde un origen irreflexivo. . . asumiendo que han llegado a sus suposiciones honestamente. ¡Espera, no tan rápido! Llevamos en nuestras mentes muchas opiniones que nos fueron alimentadas sin nuestra investigación intelectual. Los aceptamos como la lógica actual, o la vasta opinión pública, o tal vez los aprendimos de padres, amigos, maestros o medios de comunicación.

Anteriormente, en mi propia vida, estaba en marketing y promociones. Es una ciencia moderna de creación de consenso que es inteligente e insidiosa. Aprendí que el "consumidor", como tipo, reacciona emocionalmente a los mensajes. Los consumidores son realmente TODOS NOSOTROS tomados como un prototipo. Las personas como grupo forman opiniones basadas en cosas profundas y tontas.

Tendemos a estar de acuerdo con la multitud (la manada), para no molestar a las personas que nos rodean. Ya sea que seamos conscientes de esto o no, tendemos a estar de acuerdo con la camarilla entre la que deseamos ser contados.

Para que puedas agudizar tu pensamiento crítico, debes PENSAR en cómo piensas. Léalo de nuevo tantas veces como sea necesario para que tenga sentido.

Consideración e Inconsideración

Muchas personas son fuentes de información y discurso que defienden con confianza, pero sobre las que casi no han pensado. Las nociones preconcebidas abundan, de hecho, constituyen la mayor masa de opinión y actitud en nuestro mundo.

Raro es el sabio que reflexiona a través de cada pensamiento en busca de la verdad y la cohesión. Hace siglos había personas de ese tipo, eran intelectuales y reflexivos, viviendo vidas monásticas.

En nuestro apresurado mundo moderno, debemos hacernos digerir cuidadosamente la información y las opiniones sobre la marcha, disminuyendo la velocidad solo para partes importantes mientras nos quedamos boquiabiertos ante el río continuo de información diaria. ¡No es imposible! Con Internet, y con solo presionar una tecla, todos estamos conectados con el equivalente de las grandes bibliotecas de la antigüedad. Aunque, una vez más, nuestra mente reflexiva y perspicaz debe ser agudizada y aplicada para separar el trigo de la paja, el conocimiento verdadero y honesto de la propaganda. Todo está ahí.

Hay un mundo de erudición disponible para ti con el fin de agudizar tu mente.

Pero tenga esto en cuenta: Aprender a pensar es solo uno de los pasos necesarios para una mayor realización.

Consideración e Inconsideración

Claves para Pensar:

Aprende a identificar argumentos de venta ocultos.

Aprende a identificar lo irreflexivo.

Explora los bordes de la manada.

No asuma que los expertos tienen razón.

No cedas a las nociones aceptadas de la manada.

Realice sus propias autopruebas, eche un vistazo detrás de las cortinas.

Rechaza las apelaciones emocionales, son una lógica tonta.

Rechaza las apelaciones oscuras a la envidia o al odio, son injustas y autodestructivas.

Investigue por su cuenta, no "acepte la premisa".

Cuando toda la sala esté de acuerdo, deténgase y pregúntese si hay coerción.

Cuando la manada se ría al unísono, ten cuidado.

Si no tienes suficiente información para hablar, dilo.

Pide una aclaración, vuelve locos a los irreflexivos.

¡Y deja de juzgar! Esto nublará tu proceso de pensamiento y limitará tu potencial.

Consideración e Inconsideración

Las instrucciones anteriores son en realidad los principios importantes de la autoeducación, el aprendizaje intenso que se puede lograr después de sus años escolares. Incluso mis amigos con títulos avanzados de posgrado deben volver a aprender CÓMO pensar. Muchos, adultos "con educación universitaria", no han aprendido ninguna de las habilidades de CLAVES para PENSAR enumeradas anteriormente.

Con unos pocos días de práctica, puedes identificar con precisión lo reflexivo y lo irreflexivo. Dentro de un año serás un faro de (y un imán para) buenas vibraciones.

En el mundo real, la consideración es tan difícil de encontrar entre los graduados universitarios como lo es con los trabajadores de cuello azul. El pensamiento lineal y crítico es su única esperanza de ver a través de la cortina de humo de la información moderna. El pensamiento crítico, junto con una mente espiritual saludable, es lo que informa El Poder De Amar.

Piensa con claridad para amar plenamente.

Ahora que estás inmerso en el lenguaje del Amor y el Pensamiento, vamos a terminarlo.

Cómo Funciona El Poder De Amar

El Poder De Amar funciona al ver más allá de los marcadores de deficiencias terriblemente mal identificados; al ver sin juzgar a qué se opone el ego; y al identificar el propósito y la providencia a tu alrededor. Somos los conductos del Amor Infinito de... (rellene el espacio en blanco). Lo que sea que quieras llamar la fuente de nuestra creación no importa. Lo que importa es cómo concibes y percibes el mundo que te rodea y cómo eliges responder a él.

En tu vida te encontrarás con todo tipo de personas, situaciones y eventos, cada uno emparejando y vibrando a un nivel de amor. Al responder a lo que te rodea, después de un tiempo elevarás o disminuirás tu nivel personal de amor para que coincida con el que encuentres.

Si te aferras a tu nivel de amor, las personas, situaciones o eventos que encuentres se moverán para que coincidan con tu nivel. Si ni tú ni lo que encuentras cambian, habrá una división. Esto se debe a que no hay una coincidencia de niveles y la falta de armonía se vuelve demasiado grande. Esto produce la división.

Elegimos con cuánto amor vivimos, todo el día, todos los días. Elegimos si amamos de la misma manera que lo hacíamos anteriormente. A medida que vives tu vida, eliges ser como (o no te gusta), lo que encuentras.

Cómo Funciona El Poder De Amar

Dos personas pueden ver un momento simple: un niño pequeño compartiendo un regalo con su hermanita, por ejemplo. Uno ve el momento como un ejemplo precioso de la capacidad humana para amar. . . mientras que el otro solo ve ternura vacía y comenta que estos dos hermanos algún día lucharán amargamente entre sí.

Ambos observadores eligieron su reacción, conscientemente o no. Postulo que debes enfocar tu mente para elegir la primera reacción amorosa, si no eres simplemente neutral. No hace nada positivo para usted u otros ser críticos. El amor es la conciencia beneficiosa del alma humana. El amor evoluciona a la humanidad universalmente hacia arriba hacia la luz y la verdad.

Las personas son los canales a través de los cuales se manifiesta el amor universal. Esta es una cualidad trascendente de la vida humana. Esta cualidad es un anatema para la mentalidad Sinker, que tiene como objetivo (conocido por muchos y desconocido por la mayoría), degradar la cualidad trascendente del amor.

Cómo Funciona El Poder De Amar

La mentalidad Sinker es parte de la naturaleza, aunque inde-seable, ya que es contraproducente y autodestructiva. Lo que debes preguntarte es si apoyarás la mentalidad del Hundimien-to apoyando el odio y el juicio o si apoyarás la mentalidad del Pensador al Elegir el Amor y en esa elección si vivirás una vida feliz y elevada.

La opción que todos tenemos es: **"Elige el AMOR"** Esta es una frase que desarrollé para que podamos hablar todo este concepto de El Poder De Amar simplemente promoviendo esta forma de consideración. Considere los beneficios cuando "elija AMOR", y verá la clave elegante y simple para vivir una vida buena y reflexiva. La neutralidad es una forma de Amor. Ser neutral, permite un "espacio" en el que los menos reflexivos pueden evaluar su proceso actual. Ser neutral, en la mayoría de los casos, niega el juicio algo contra lo que despotricar.

La imagen de una mano sosteniendo esos tres dedos en partic-ular es un recordatorio de las opciones que cada persona tiene para responder al mundo. Esta comunicación icónica recuerda rápidamente a todos que solo hay tres opciones con las que responder a sus percepciones. ("Me Encanta", "Lo Odio" o "Lo Que Sea")

Cómo Funciona El Poder De Amar

Aquí hay un diálogo simple que uno puede usar para iniciar una conversación discutiendo la idea de **"Elegir AMOR"**.

Digamos que acabas de ver a alguien actuar de una manera que se describiría mejor como irreflexiva. Si parecen accesibles y no hay amenaza de violencia física, puedes hablar con ellos, en voz baja, uno a uno, y así es como podrían ir las cosas:

Tú: Oye (hablado con calma), ¿sabes qué es esto? (Pides esto levantando tres dedos. Ahora, el individuo irreflexivo tiene las mismas tres opciones que siempre tendrá cuando te pares frente a ellos levantando tu mano).

Ellos: No, ¿qué quieres decir? (Al escuchar su voz, escuchará "Me Encanta", "Lo Odio" o "Lo Que Sea").

Tú: Esto es magia. ¿Te gustaría aprender la magia que creará una felicidad ilimitada en tu vida?

Ellos: (Una vez más, se les pide que respondan a su pregunta y lo harán, de las tres opciones). Bien. (Es una opción y de nuevo se puede escuchar su disposición en el tono de su voz. La única otra cosa que pueden decir es: "No").

Cómo Funciona El Poder De Amar

Tú: Este es un recordatorio de que cada vez que respondemos a las cosas que nos rodean, nuestras acciones serán abrazadoras, rechazadas o neutrales. Ahora la magia se encuentra en recordar que cuando rechazamos nos disminuimos a nosotros mismos. Rechazar a alguien, algo o una situación nos degrada al crear resistencia y fricción. La gente se acostumbra, pero todavía nos arrastra hacia abajo y no tiene por qué ser así. Podemos hacer cosas positivas y edificantes que nos traerán más felicidad. Lo sé, eso suena un poco trippy, pero ¿de qué otra manera podemos describirlo? Ser crítico no puede crear felicidad.

Aquí es cuando les das una sonrisa. El concepto es que esto les ayude a pensar en cómo piensan. Has hecho tu parte.

ESA ES TODA LA HISTORIA, LA PRÁCTICA HACE LA PERFECCIÓN Y UNA VEZ QUE TE HAYAS ALEJADO DE ELEGIR EL JUICIO, "ODIO", VERÁS COSAS QUE SOLÍAN MOLESTARTE BAJO UNA LUZ COMPLETAMENTE NUEVA, O NO TE MOLESTAN EN ABSOLUTO. CUANDO BUSCAMOS ELEVAR TODO LO QUE NOS RODEA, NUESTRA FELICIDAD SE EXPANDIRÁ NATURALMENTE.

Ustedes, y el mundo,
se benefician al abrazar,
comprometerse y encarnar
El Poder De Amar.

Gracias.

Davida Patrick Moore (el autor)

Como consultor esotérico, Davida Patrick Moore realiza los oficios
de la adivinación, la meditación y la sanación energética, junto con
la consultoría y el entrenamiento
en los ámbitos de la manifestación,
la gestión personal del sistema de
energía, la gestión y la salud. y más
claramente en la dinámica social y
cultural. Astrólogo Profesional, Tarotis-
ta, y Sanador Pránico certificado, son
aclarados en la biografía de Davida.
Otros créditos incluyen; rock/pop,
jazz, y músico clásico, entrenador/en-
trenador esotérico, orador público, y
autor publicado.

Consciente En los años sesenta, el
interés de Davida por lo esotérico y
cósmico eran expresiones naturales
desde una edad temprana. En su ju-

Davida Patrick Moore

ventud, las civilizaciones antiguas tocaron un acorde dentro de Davida;
la cultura, el lenguaje y el mito eran atracciones curiosas. Un esbozo
aproximado de compromiso va desde la música clásica, la meditación y
la astrología / tarot, a través de la filosofía espiritual, la publicación y la
comunicación y hablando en público, a sanador energético, entrenador
esotérico y entrenador. "Thinkers and Sinkers, Why Are They Trying
To Kivll You?" El libro de Davida de 2011, (ThinkersAndSinkers.com),
describe los patrones interpersonales que se encuentran en cada nivel
de la vida y en el quid de la experiencia moderna. La expresión de la
intención beligerante encontrada a lo largo de los paisajes sociales y
personales expone la lucha existencial contra el Amor Universal por
Caos. Revelar esta influencia autodestructiva es primordial para los
esfuerzos de la vida de Davida. Apoyar el crecimiento espiritual y la
autosanación son el enfoque central de estos esfuerzos.